Teleworking
for Library
and Information
Professionals

Routledge
Taylor & Francis Group

LONDON AND NEW YORK

THE ASSOCIATION FOR INFORMATION MANAGEMENT

imi   INFORMATION MANAGEMENT INTERNATIONAL

First published 1999 by Aslib
The Association for Information Management and
Information Managment International

Published 2015 by Routledge
2 Park Square, Milton Park, Abingdon, Oxon OX14 4RN
711 Third Avenue, New York, NY 10017, USA

*Routledge is an imprint of the Taylor & Francis Group,
an informa business*

ISBN 978-0-85142-416-3 (pbk)

Teleworking
for Library
and Information
Professionals

Monica Blake

Routledge
Taylor & Francis Group

LONDON AND NEW YORK

 THE ASSOCIATION FOR INFORMATION MANAGEMENT

 INFORMATION MANAGEMENT INTERNATIONAL

Is your organisation a corporate member of Aslib?

Aslib, The Association for Information Management is a world class corporate membership organisation with over 2000 members in some 70 countries. Aslib actively promotes best practice in the management of information resources. It lobbies on all aspects of the management of, and legislation concerning, information at local, national and international levels.

Aslib provides consultancy and information services, professional development training, conferences, specialist recruitment, Internet products, and publishes primary and secondary journals, conference proceedings, directories and monographs.

Series Editor

Sylvia Webb is a well known consultant, author and lecturer in the information management field. Her first book, *Creating an Information Service*, now in its third edition, was published by Aslib and has sold in over forty countries. She has experience of working in both the public and private sectors, ranging from public libraries to national and international organisations. She has also been a lecturer at Ashridge Management College, specialising in management and interpersonal skills, which led to her second book, *Personal Development in Information Work*, also published by Aslib. She has served on a number of government advisory bodies and is past Chair of the Information and Library Services Lead Body which develops National Vocational Qualifications (NVQs) for the LIS profession. She is actively involved in professional education with Aslib and the Library Association and is also a former Vice-President of the Institute of Information Scientists. As well as being editor of this series, Sylvia Webb has written three of the Know How Guides: *Making a charge for library and information services*, *Preparing a guide to your library and information service* and *Knowledge management: linchpin of change*.

A complete listing of all titles in the series can be found at the back of this volume.

Acknowledgements

I am extremely grateful to all those people who agreed to allow their experiences of teleworking to be presented as case studies, including: Juliet Amissah, Phil Bradley, Lynne Clitheroe, Nicola Harrison, Justus Krabshuis, Alison Scammell, Peter Williams and participants in the Goldsmiths' Library of Economic Literature Catalogue Retroconversion Project at the University of London Library.

Thank you also to respondents to a message on the LIS-LINK listserv who provided pointers towards useful information: John Lindsay (School of Information Systems at Kingston University), Rebecca Linley (Centre for the Public Library in the Information Society at the University of Sheffield), and Patrick Overy (EDC Librarian, University of Exeter). And thank you to Alan Denbigh of the Telework Telecottage and Telecentre Association (TCA) for sending me details of a survey of members' needs and to Guy Daines of the Library Association for leaflets on self-employment and teleworking.

Finally I would like to thank David Martyn and Alison Scammell for reading early drafts of the manuscript, and the series editor Sylvia Webb for sending helpful material during the writing of the guide and for her patience in awaiting the final version.

Contents

1. Introduction

This guide is intended as an introduction to teleworking for library and information professionals. It considers teleworking among LIS staff as well as teleworkers as users of LIS services. The first three chapters provide a general account of teleworking – what it is, how to manage it, and issues to consider when doing it from home. Chapters 4, 5 and 6 are directed specifically towards the LIS community. Chapter 4 suggests teleworking opportunities for LIS professionals, and Chapter 5 gives case studies of LIS professionals who are already, or have been, teleworking. Chapter 6 highlights the kinds of information needed by teleworkers and looks at the potential role of libraries in developing services for teleworkers. The final chapters provide a resource for further information.

But what do we mean by teleworking?

Terminology

The definition of teleworking used here is a broad one: 'working at a distance from one's employer or client, generally using information technology resources'. It is characterised by moving the work to the workers, instead of the workers to work. Some writers restrict the term to employees; others specify the amount of time worked away from the organisation and/or the nature of communication (e.g. electronic) with the organisation.

'Telecommuting', 'flexiplace working', 'location-independent working', 'distance working', 'remote working' and 'alternative officing' are common synonyms of 'teleworking', although some people only use 'telecommuting' when there is evidence that it has actually replaced commuting. Telecommuting is more frequently used in North America.

Teleworking is a type of flexible working. Others are job-sharing and flexitime, part-time and term-time working. Homeworking means working at or from home. Often it is synonymous with teleworking, but not all teleworkers work at home and not all homeworkers are teleworkers. Teleworking includes working at a local telecottage or telecentre – where workers have access to information technology and some office support facilities – instead of commuting to an office. Sometimes the expression 'traditional homeworking' is used to refer to people doing such work as knitting, making toys and stuffing envelopes.

There is much overlap between the terms telecottage and telecentre. Some ten years ago, telecottages tended to be community-based facilities providing local communities with access to technology, training and work. Telecentres were more likely to be established for specific commercial purposes. For telecottages, the emphasis was on social support for their users, while telecentres focused more on providing a well-managed, secure and uninterrupted working environment for people needing a place where they can get on with the job and be easily connected to their employer or client. Today such distinctions are becoming blurred.

Some of the services associated with telecottages and telecentres are now being offered by business centres, especially in urban areas. The Virtual Office Group, for example, advertises serviced offices with advanced communications technology in Central London. It is aimed at businesses practising new ways of working (*http://www.voffice.com*).

Types of teleworking

Teleworking can be carried out at home or in a telecottage, telecentre, satellite branch office or – in the case of peripatetic (mobile) teleworkers – in a car or hotel room. Teleworkers may be employees or self-employed. They may spend all their working time away from their employer's or client's premises, or may telework for one or two days a week.

Huws (1997) identifies five types of teleworking:

- multi-site teleworking, where an employee alternates between the employer's premises and other sites such as the home;

- tele-homeworking, where the teleworker is based exclusively in the home, and works for a single employer;

- freelance or independent teleworking, where work is wholly based in or from the home and carried out on a freelance basis for a variety of different clients rather than a single employer;

- mobile teleworkers, whereby workers spend much of their working time on a variety of different sites, such as customers' premises, and use portable equipment to keep in touch with the employer (for example, sales representatives and inspectors); and

- re-located back office teleworking, which involves activities carried out at a distance from the employer's headquarters but on premises owned by the employer (such as data entry and telephone banking).

This guide is concerned with varieties of the first three types – those which are most likely to be relevant to the library and information community.

New ways to work

Interest in teleworking has arisen as a response to a number of circumstances: the oil crisis of 1973, fewer people working in manufacturing and more having information-related jobs, downsizing and re-engineering of organisations during the 1980s, and new thinking about patterns of living and working. Throughout the period computers and telecommunications have expanded their capabilities while their costs have come down. Thus teleworking becomes ever more feasible.

In the United States, writers like Jack Nilles et al. (1976) saw teleworking as a way of reducing fuel consumption in the wake of the oil crisis. Nilles estimated that if one in seven urban commuters dropped out, the country would have no need to import oil. Such ideas were popularised by Alvin

Toffler (1981), particularly in his book *The Third Wave*. Toffler described how the industrial phase of civilisation (the Second Wave) was giving way to the information age (the Third Wave), and predicted that increasing numbers of people would take up teleworking.

As companies shed workers during the 1980s, many people became self employed and some adopted teleworking. Handy (1990) has described this trend in terms of organisations needing greater flexibility to expand and contract their services to meet customer demand. To do this they would use a central core of professionals and managers who work full time for the organisation, a contractual fringe to which work is outsourced, and a flexible workforce made up of temporary or part-time workers.

Kinsman (1987, 1991) draws on research by Taylor Nelson Applied Futures to show that increasing numbers of people are more concerned about leading fulfilled lives than about material gain. He believes such people will be attracted to teleworking because of the potential benefits it offers in terms of flexibility, independence, job satisfaction and reduced commuting.

In the 1990s several trends are evident. More women are working. People in full-time employment are working longer hours and often taking work home. There are stories of downshifting, along with concerns about the environment. Downshifting is defined as moving out of the fast lane of a career (e.g. by taking up voluntary simplicity – including working less and earning less –

in search of a more satisfactory way of life). Architects are building more homes containing offices, and are predicting that the workplace will be used for meeting colleagues and entertaining clients while tasks requiring undisturbed concentration will be carried out at home (e.g. Leaman & Borden 1993). Lloyd (1993) even suggested that by the end of this century having an office at home could be as vital and as common as having a kitchen.

The 'virtual office' is forecast to become the norm in many industries (Taylor 1998), a trend facilitated by growth in the use of email and intranets. Some companies are adopting 'hot desking' or 'hotelling', whereby workspace is shared with colleagues working at different times. Employees do not have their own workstations, but are allocated a place to work when they show up at the office. They have lockers or mobile filing cabinets for personal storage, and a computer system routes phone calls and email as necessary.

A report from the European Commission (1998) states that telework has now reached a critical point of take-off where it is becoming mainstream in information-rich sectors and jobs and for skilled and high level personnel. The authors predict that, 'Over the next few years, the take up of telework can be expected to spread throughout other sectors and jobs as part of the unfolding of the global networked economy and the widespread growth of virtual organisations and teams'. The term 'virtual organisation' can refer either to an organisation without physical premises but where most of the interaction is electronic or to a temporary group of freelancers brought together to work on a specific project (Scammell 1998).

Teleworking in the UK

Early examples of teleworking in the UK are F International (now the FI Group) and CPS (a division of ICL). F International was founded in 1962 by Steve (Stephanie) Shirley, a computer programmer who wanted to combine family and career. This software company – originally known as Freelance Programmers – has aimed to develop the unutilised intellectual energy of individuals and groups unable to work in a conventional environment. Many of its workers are women with family responsibilities.

CPS dates from 1969, when ICL was in urgent need of software planners and analysts. Hilary Cropper, at that time a divisional director of ICL, embarked on a pilot homeworking project with a team of women who had previously been with ICL but had left to have families. The scheme was successful, and what was then known as Contract Programming Services grew steadily to about 60 people in 1974 and branched out into software support, technical writing and applications development. In 1978 a separate group, Product Maintenance Support (PMS), was formed to handle the software support function. Hilary Cropper later moved on to F International.

In the early 1980s, teleworking initiatives were introduced by Rank Xerox and the Department of Trade and Industry. The former scheme involved ex-employees setting up their own limited companies and working for Rank Xerox on a contract basis. The DTI Remote Work Units Project was set up as part of a plan to use IT to help people with disabilities. This project involved equipping disabled people from different organisations with personal computers and allowing them to work from home. The tasks undertaken included typesetting, tachograph analysis, financial management and viewdata editing.

Crossaig, based at Helensburgh in Scotland, is a well documented case of an organisation that makes considerable use of teleworkers (Blaxter 1995). The company provides services for electronic publishing, in particular working with secondary publishers to create electronic databases using advanced production processes. For example, it arranges abstracting and indexing of biomedical articles for Elsevier's Embase database. Crossaig teleworkers receive OCR-scanned images of journal articles via ISDN links. Teleworking permits the company to gain access to skilled people beyond the Helensburgh area and provides work for teleworkers who often live in remote areas.

Teleworking is now practised in a range of organisations – especially financial services (like Allied Dunbar, Lloyds TSB and Scottish Widows) and IT companies (such as BT and Digital) but also Asda, British Airways and the Open University. Publishers have often used teleworkers, for example as freelance editors and designers; this trend escalated during downsizing within the industry during the 1980s (Stanworth *et al.* 1993).

A number of local authorities, such as Enfield Borough Council, used teleworking to cope with the additional administrative burden required by the introduction of the UK's poll tax (now the Council tax). More recently local authorities have introduced teleworking schemes to discourage use of cars for commuting. In 1996, Surrey County Council opened a telecentre at Epsom. Available for use by all Council employees, the telecentre's facilities include an open plan area with desks and PCs, quiet rooms, meeting rooms, kitchen facilities and a free car park (*http://www.surreycc.gov.uk/ telecentre*). Bertin & Denbigh (1998) list 19 local authorities using teleworkers in Britain in August 1997.

The government has begun collecting telework data as part of its routine Labour Force Survey. The spring 1997 survey reported that 987,000 people (4% of those in employment) were teleworkers in their main job. Of these teleworkers, 70% were managers, administrators, professionals and associate professionals.

A survey for BT, also in 1997, found that while only 6% of organisations had any formal approach to teleworking, 49% had some kind of informal arrangement; 18% of organisations were likely to introduce some kind of scheme within the next five years. Among large organisations (employing more than 1000 people), three-quarters had some kind of flexible working in place (European Commission 1998).

9

Benefits and drawbacks of teleworking

Teleworking can provide a powerful solution to a number of workplace problems. It is effective for some people in some situations, but it is not a universal panacea. It provides opportunities, but also presents risks. There are pros and cons for both teleworkers and employers.

Teleworking allows greater flexibility in time and place, enabling workers to retain work after relocation and more easily achieve a balance between work and family. It can provide work in remote areas and enhance opportunities for people with disabilities. Many teleworkers report greater job satisfaction than non-teleworkers and are less likely to suffer repetitive strain injury (RSI) as they can take more frequent breaks. Teleworking can improve the quality of life by satisfying the desire for autonomy, escaping from office politics, and reducing the amount of time spent travelling.

One of the greatest benefits of teleworking to employers is the greater productivity that results from reduction of distractions, reduced commuting so staff can be available for work at a given time irrespective of travel conditions and weather, reduced time off for sickness and increased flexibility. In addition, teleworking enables employers to retain valued staff, access a wider pool of skills, and reduce office overheads or avoid moving to larger premises.

Nicolle (1998) reports that companies such as British Gas, Barclays and Xerox were saving up to

£1000 a head a year in office costs by equipping staff with PCs and links to central systems and switchboards so that they could work from home or while out on the road.

Teleworking can facilitate disaster recovery. When one of Digital's offices burnt to the ground, creative application of telework had business systems fully operational within 48 hours (Skyrme 1993). In Los Angeles there was a dramatic increase in teleworking in the aftermath of the earthquake there in 1994.

The reduction in commuting benefits the environment by cutting levels of pollution and decreasing the amount of traffic congestion. The environmental charity World Wide Fund for Nature uses teleworking to cut down on travel throughout the world.

On the down side, the most frequently reported problem is isolation. This can include lack of social contact as well as inability to easily discuss professional issues with colleagues or exchange hints in dealing with aspects of the job such as software idiosyncrasies. Professional isolation may be alleviated by strategies like networking, for instance by being active in professional organisations or attending conferences. Managers of teleworkers should actively develop good communications with teleworkers (see chapter 2). Social isolation is a more complex issue, as it may be inherent in the reason for the adoption of teleworking, for instance staying at home with a sick relative or moving to a new area to be with a relocated partner. While teleworking may provide an attractive alternative

11

to conventional work, it may act as a disincentive to dealing with the isolation involved.

Some teleworkers fear reduced career prospects. Employed teleworkers may feel they will not get the same opportunities for promotion because they may not be informed when vacancies occur. They need to ensure that their skills are kept up to date and that they are not left out of more general training programmes. Moon & Stanworth (1997) report a flexible worker complaining that the training he received was 'task specific and on-the-job, not skill learning but task training'.

Unions are concerned there may be an erosion of the forms of worker protection that have been negotiated over the years. Sometimes teleworking involves a move to self-employment and the accompanying risks and responsibilities such as earning an adequate income, insuring against sickness and incapacity, and contributing to a pension fund.

The ability to spend more time with the family may not always contribute to harmony in the home. While it is a bonus to some teleworkers, others find it difficult to establish clear boundaries between work and home life; the increasing interpenetration of work and domestic life can cause new stresses and damage to family life. This is more likely to be the case if the teleworker does not have a separate room for work.

From the employer's point of view, the main problem with teleworking is the difficulty of management. Many managers have negative attitudes towards teleworking although surveys show this is more prevalent in organisations without teleworkers than among those who have tried it. A BT project found that middle management resistance to change was a far greater obstacle than the technical issues which had to be overcome.

Some employers are concerned that the isolation of teleworkers will lead to damage to corporate culture. Sometimes workers who are not teleworking have to take on more run of the mill tasks in the office because fewer people are available. Security is often perceived as risk. Generally, carrying out a trial will identify risks so that appropriate measures can be taken.

Huws (1997) points to a number of more general risks arising from teleworking. She fears 'social dumping' will result from the export of jobs across national boundaries, and a growing polarisation of the workforce between a protected core of (predominantly male) full-time, permanent employees with access to continuing staff development and employer-provided benefits, and a (predominantly female) periphery of casual workers who lack access to training, pensions and other benefits and are largely excluded from representation within the social dialogue.

2. Management Issues

Implementation

Much teleworking is carried out on an ad hoc or tacit basis – such as individuals working away from the office to complete a report, or companies allowing certain employees to work at home at their own discretion and expense. However, large organisations introducing teleworking on a planned basis adopt a formal approach involving a feasibility study, a pilot project and monitoring and evaluation of the pilot. Initial stages involve identifying jobs suitable for teleworking (see also Chapter 4) and selecting members of staff for the pilot project.

Analysing whether a job is appropriate for teleworking involves looking at what function the job serves: whether work is performed over the telephone, in person or via computer; and the amount of time the employee needs to spend in direct contact with colleagues and users.

Teleworkers should be self-motivated, self-disciplined, well-organised, show initiative, be good communicators, good time managers, able to cope with lack of social contact, computer literate, good decision makers, and effective problem solvers. Maitland (1998) recommends that they should also be adaptable and able to compromise; technically self-sufficient; knowledgeable about the way in which the organisation works; oriented towards results; and able to survive without regular chats

15

with colleagues. Where an organisation makes use of self-employed teleworkers, criteria like reliability and 'professional attitude towards job' gain in importance (Korte & Wynne 1996).

Home-based teleworking may not be feasible if space is at a premium in the home of a potential teleworker. In some teleworking schemes, managers inspect the premises, checking that there is adequate working space along with space to store work and equipment. The home needs to be secure against fire and theft and meet any statutory business health and safety requirements. Where appropriate, child care arrangements should be in place. Some of these issues can be considered by conducting focus groups for potential teleworkers.

In addition to the conditions mentioned above, prerequisites for the implementation of teleworking include: support of top management; openness to innovation; identification of needs that can be met through teleworking; adequate start-up and continuing funding sources; and the availability of information and back-up equipment. Managers should be able to set clear goals and be ready to measure output not by hours but by the quality of work and whether deadlines are met. Some companies prefer new staff not to telework until they have a good grasp of how the organisation works.

Teleworking should always be voluntary – i.e. agreed with the person concerned. Maitland (1998) emphasises the importance of making sure that potential teleworkers 'know exactly what they are in for'.

A pilot project provides an opportunity to test and tune policies and procedures and to assess the impact on the organisation. The pilot will need a project manager and clear responsibilities and reporting arrangements. Parameters to assess the success of the pilot will need to be developed.

Guidelines

When setting up a telework operation, it can be useful to adopt guidelines to clarify the responsibilities of both teleworkers and their managers. Huws (1997) provides separate guidelines to cover each of the types of teleworking outlined in Chapter 1, and highlights examples of good practice among organisations employing teleworkers.

Gray *et al.* (1993) present guidelines to help managers commence and successfully operate a homeworking arrangement. In addition to recommendations on selecting the homeworker, job requirements, personal requirements and the home environment, these guidelines cover equipment, insurance, pay and conditions, and taxation. The authors point out that most companies expect a teleworking arrangement to be cost-effective and that managers of potential teleworkers should produce a detailed business case justifying the proposal. The business case should include office costs, equipment, heating and lighting costs, terms and conditions, communications costs, administrative costs, and work output.

The guidelines list a number of management responsibilities. Managers must consider the impact of the introduction of a homeworking arrangment on their job and the jobs of others. In particular, they should:

- make regular visits to the homeworker's home;
- check the impact of the homeworker's absence on the work of office-based employees;
- brief other affected employees; and
- establish working, reporting and communication arrangements between the homeworker, management and other colleagues.

Gray *et al.* specify that procedures are required for:

- emergency contact arrangements;
- how sickness and accidents will be reported;
- how expenses will be claimed;
- how faults with equipment are reported;
- ensuring that the homeworker does not become isolated from the company and colleagues;
- monitoring the performance of the homeworker;
- ensuring that the homeworker attends any necessary training courses;
- learning how to use new communications technology; and
- ensuring that the homeworker is counselled on the position regarding career development.

A number of unions have issued guidelines for the introduction of teleworking. The public service union Unison (*http://www.unison.org.uk/polres/telework.htm*) has produced a checklist for negotiating arrangements with employers of home-based teleworkers:

- Telework should always be voluntary.
- Teleworkers should be employees (with full employment rights) not self-employed subcontractors.
- Teleworkers should operate from a separate room in the home, examined by qualified health and safety experts.
- There should be regular opportunities for workers to meet each other, as well as office-based colleagues.
- Teleworkers should have access to email and telephone links.
- Teleworkers should be assigned a particular manager who would ensure regular contact.
- Teleworkers should have the same rates of pay and other employment benefits as office-based workers.
- Teleworkers should be included in the career development programme of the organisation.
- All equipment should be supplied and maintained by the employer.
- Financial arrangements should be in place to cover extra costs such as lighting and heating.

- Employers should be responsible for health and safety; health and safety visits should be regular.
- Teleworkers should have their own representatives on the organisation's health and safety committees.
- Teleworkers should enjoy the same rights as other workers to join trade unions and have their own representatives.
- Employees who transfer from office to home-based working should be entitled to a trial period and should have a right to return to previous arrangements.
- All teleworkers should be entitled to an annual review of arrangements.

MSF (Manufacturing, Science and Finance) and the banking union BIFU have similar sets of guidelines. The MSF code of practice for employers who are introducing teleworking into an organisation is available at *http://www.msf.org.uk*. BIFU specifies that no 'spy in the house' camera or key depression monitoring equipment is to be fitted to a homeworker's VDU.

Despite a difference of emphasis between union and managers' guidelines, there is agreement that clear decisions should be reached in advance on such topics as provision and maintenance of equipment, career development, and health and safety. The issues raised by the guidelines indicate the range of considerations associated with teleworking.

An electronic handbook on implementing telework (http://www.telework-mirti.org/handbook/inglese/2checker.htm) recommends that contracts for teleworkers should include clauses on the following topics:

- employment status;
- voluntary principle;
- working place(s)
- health and safety;
- acquisition, installation and maintenance of the equipment, costs of new lines;
- working hours;
- management and supervision;
- training;
- indemnity;
- insurance policy;
- right to representation; and
- termination.

The State of Utah's Telecommuting handbook provides an example of a typical contract between employer and teleworker (http://www.governor.state.ut.us/sitc/telecom.htm).

Communication

With isolation being a potential drawback of teleworking, effective communications are essential. Huws (1996) considers good communications as 'perhaps the single most important key to success in teleworking'.

Sheehy & Gallagher (1996) maintain: 'Communication is more than a medium for work or a by-product of organizational life. Talk is the psychological glue that makes work possible. Organizations are created and maintained through the talk of their members.'

Inevitably teleworking involves fewer face-to-face meetings than occur within the organisation. Nilles (1994) has observed that novice telemanagers are concerned that the loss in communications richness – from facial expression, body language and voice – will be so high that they will have difficulties getting their ideas across to their employees.

The art is in selecting appropriate technology for particular kinds of communication. While the telephone is most useful for urgent communication, services like email, fax and the post are more suitable for detailed material or for routine messages. Where communication is interactive, then face-to-face meetings, telephone or videoconferencing technology is most appropriate. Maitland (1998) warns against relying too heavily on one-way emails, saying it is better to use a mix of telephone, videoconferencing and face-to-face meetings. She also advises against using technology to deliver bad news.

Gray *et al.* (1993) consider simultaneity of communication. For communication at the same time in different places (remote meetings), they recommend audioconferencing, videoconferencing and screen sharing. As appropriate technology for messaging (different times, different places), they suggest voice and electronic messaging, computer conferencing, shared calendars, group writing and shared databases.

If videoconferencing is used, training may be needed to get the best results. Many systems are somewhat jerky, which means learning to moderate body language. Often it is only possible for one person to speak at a time, so participants need to develop gestures to indicate when they have finished making a point.

Managers of teleworkers evolve strategies for keeping teleworkers in touch with developments in the organisation. For example, they might invite teleworkers to social events or circulate publications to them. They may encourage them to use the corporate intranet facilities. For large teleworking schemes, it can be worthwhile to produce newsletters and audio or videocassettes specially for the teleworkers in the organisation.

Training

In a constantly changing workplace environment, training is a crucial issue. For teleworkers, it can be of even greater significance.

Teleworkers need not only to be proficient at their jobs, they also require a number of other skills. In addition to computer literacy and good time management, teleworkers need good interpersonal skills to develop effective working relationships without face-to-face meetings.

Self-employed teleworkers need to be able to market a service to a distant client and to manage a remote client. They have to be able to use telecommunications economically and choose telecommunications to suit the services they offer. It is also useful to know about the legal and regulatory framework concerned with teleworking.

Employed teleworkers need training to prepare them for working from home, including health and safety training. Huws (1997) recommends that training be carried out in person. She emphasises that teleworkers should not be expected to train themselves from manuals when on-site staff are given face-to-face tuition. All kinds of teleworkers need training to update existing IT skills and acquire new ones. Managers and teleworkers should receive training in effective communication methods.

People who have been teleworking for a number of years recognise a need for training in the management of virtual organisations (Bertin & Denbigh 1998). The subjects that need to be covered include project management, effective use of email, videoconferencing, groupware tools, file transfer, recruitment and management of staff at distant locations and the conduct of face-to-face meetings between teleworking teams. Apgar (1998) believes that managers should re-educate people about what used to be intuitive aspects of office life: when they should work, how often they should communicate, whether to talk or type, and what to say when they do. He says, 'From an early age, we learn how to live in organizations at particular locations. In the alternative workplace, we have to learn to be in and of the organization while not being at it.'

Some courses have been developed especially for teleworkers. A vocational qualification in teleworking, which is due to become an NVQ/SNVQ in late 1998, is certified by City and Guilds of London Institute and by the Scottish Qualification Authority. It was developed under the Teleworking for Europe project, a partnership between Staffordshire TEC, Leek College and Staffordshire County Council. The scheme was part-funded by the EU under the Euroform programme, and developed at Moorlands Telecottage.

The qualification is intended to equip the candidate with a platform of competence on which a service or skill can be overlaid. Course units include: setting up and configuring a computer system; telecommunications and data transmission; information processing; text processing; and self management.

Many courses are available for study at home, but outside courses provide a good opportunity for remote workers to get out of the house and to meet other people. Training may also be given by on-the-job instruction, by a specialist trainer or by the manager, or it may take the form of coaching.

Teleworkers might find they need to learn to use new software packages or to acquire particular business skills. TECs (Training and Enterprise Councils) provide many such courses, some specifically targetted at people who are unemployed. Other possibilities include further education colleges, telecottages, enterprise agencies or private providers. A number of organisations offer training on email and the Internet. For people wishing to experiment with the Internet in a supportive environment, there are a number of cybercafes and cyberpubs in the UK, and increasingly libraries are providing opportunities to explore software packages or learn about the Internet (see also Chapter 6). Organisations like Aslib, the Library Association, Informed Business Services and TFPL offer not only Internet courses but also courses on a range of topics of relevance to the professional development of the LIS worker.

The contract between the management and remote worker should help determine who pays for what. If the training intervention benefits both parties, then it would be reasonable to negotiate sharing of costs. If training is offered by management as a means to attract potential remote workers, then management might judge this to be a reasonable part of recruitment costs.

Curran & Williams (1997) point out that it is in management's best interest to encourage remote workers to continue their learning and development, and recommend that this is best done by management adopting a coaching style. In particular, management should look for opportunities to provide feedback, and for work tasks that stretch the remote worker, mixing routine tasks with the developmental ones. Management should try to adopt a work style that encourages the remote worker to say how best the work could be done, to identify potential problems and to offer contingency plans.

Nilles (1994) believes that training is necessary not only for teleworking employees and their managers, but also for non-teleworkers with whom they deal regularly such as non-teleworking colleagues and the families of home-based teleworkers. For home-based teleworkers, Nilles recommends the following types of training: scheduling work periods, accepting shifts in household responsibilities, controlling interruptions, and resisting temptations.

Managers need to learn how to manage teleworkers. This may include adopting the management style of monitoring by results instead of by process, setting performance standards and guidelines for remote work, and troubleshooting. Communication is a vital issue. Instructions must be more complete when they cannot be continually amended. Managers have to ensure that desired results are clearly and fully stated.

Telework training in the LIS context has been described by Davenport & Wormell (1997), who collaborated on a joint course between Queen Margaret College in Scotland and the Royal School of Librarianship in Denmark. This ambitious project introduced undergraduate students to tools and issues that are relevant to teleworking. The course designers identified a list of tasks as measures of competence to telework. Students were asked to:

- prepare home pages which present both personal and professional profiles;
- establish contact and negotiate responsibilities with a remote working partner;
- design a business plan over a period of weeks with this partner;
- identify online sources for project work;

- identify sources of information about macro-level trends in society and the future of work; and
- identify sources of advice to equip themselves as teleworkers.

Competence in these tasks was considered to be indicative of experience in the managerial areas of: coordinating tasks; managing time frames for group projects; resolving questions of responsibility, accountability and ownership; management of information to support project work; tendering and costing issues for network work; and marketing.

Technical competence was indicated by: presentation of the self (e.g. student's own profile and style of presentation)on the Internet; working knowledge of a groupware application; online searching skills; organising and management of jointly accessed local and remote files; and archiving and storing project work.

3. A Workstation in the Home

Space

Equipped with a laptop computer and a mobile phone, a teleworker can work anywhere. And many do. But most teleworkers also require some physical space set aside for their work. For a great many, this space is in the home.

The home will need to have enough space for undisturbed work and a safe work area. In some homes it is possible to put aside a room to use as an office (the ideal scenario), while in others a part of a room has to suffice. If a separate office is not an option, a room that is not in daily use – such as a guest bedroom – is preferable to one used frequently by other residents of the home. Some houses have unused space that would lend itself to conversion like an attic, conservatory or even part of a wide landing or large entrance hall. If part of a room is to be used as a work space, it may be possible to divide the room using a screen or curtain. Mack (1995) and Paul (1996) provide a number of stylish and imaginative examples of home offices.

In the UK, working in the garden is not feasible for much of the year. However, some teleworkers set up offices in their garage or in specially designed outhouses installed in the garden. The company Homelodge specialises in single-storey timber lodges, which are serviced with electricity and have lights, power points and a heater. TempleCo Ten's Home Office is a modular structure with insulated walls, roof and floor. This self-contained workspace is double-glazed and prewired for light and power; it includes an electric heater, telephone sockets, television point and a burglar alarm. Portakabin sells and leases stand-alone accommodation that is suitable for home offices.

Key considerations include security, storage facilities, comfort and convenience. These factors will be affected by other residents of the home as well as by visitors. A number of issues relate to security. First there is confidentiality of work. It may be necessary to lock material away from people who have no right to see it. Second there is the possibility of fire or burglary. A home office contains much valuable equipment and adequate precautions need to be taken to protect it (see also Insurance below). Work in progress is also of value – fireproof cabinets and backup procedures have a role to play. Third it may be necessary to protect work from the attentions of children and animals.

When setting up an office in the home, it is important to achieve a balance between the pragmatics of standard office equipment and the aesthetics of home. An attractive environment can improve productivity by lifting the spirits, increasing confidence and enhancing enjoyment of work. Colour can alter a room's apparent temperature and size, and affect the mood.

Equipment and supplies

The equipment needed for teleworking will depend on the nature of the job and on facilities available locally. The main hardware items for the home office are personal computer, telephone (including an answering machine) and modem. Others include fax, scanner and photocopier. For those travelling a lot, a laptop computer and mobile phone are useful.

For equipment that is used only occasionally, it may be more cost effective to pay for use as needed. Most local communities have photocopying facilities and often fax is available in newsagents and libraries. Business Links and some telecottages are introducing facilities for videoconferencing – a technology where the cost is decreasing and the quality improving.

A second telephone line is advisable – either to keep business calls separate from personal calls, or to allow simultaneous use of telephone and the Internet. With ISDN (Integrated Services Digital Network), a number of devices can share the same line. However, this technology is not yet widespread. If it does achieve greater penetration, it will allow more teamwork among teleworkers, as tasks which normally require a physical meeting become possible at a distance through collaborative working software, fast transfer of large files, and high quality voice communication (Bertin & Denbigh 1998).

Furniture begins with a desk and chair. The work surface should be high enough that one does not have to bend over it, with plenty of clearance underneath – generally some 63-76 cm from the floor. A keyboard should be placed at lap level – about 5-6 cm below the work surface so that the forearms and wrists fall in a straight horizontal plane during typing. The chair should be adjustable and have a seat that can be moved up and down to suit the height of the desk. Thighs should be parallel to the floor and feet flat on the floor or on a foot rest. Well designed office chairs have five legs – making for stability – and a swivel mechanism.

Good lighting makes for more effective work. Task lighting, which provides strong illumination centred on the immediate work area, is usually in the form of a desk lamp, preferably one that can be rotated to throw light where it is most needed. In a multipurpose room, task lighting can define a work area visually. Background lighting softens the potentially harsh contrast between the pool of light on the work area and darkness around it. Whether using natural or artificial light, it is important to avoid working in one's own shadow; thus a work area should be lit from the left for right-handed people and vice versa.

Even where computers are used extensively, a home office generates an enormous quantity of paper. This requires storage space – filing cabinets and files of every description (hanging files, box files, Lever Arch files etc). Shelves are needed to store books, journals and manuals as well as work in progress and box files, and cupboards for stationery and packing materials. Disks are best stored in fireproof containers.

Regulations

Health and safety

Under the Health and Safety at Work Act 1974, employers have a duty to protect the health, safety and welfare of their employees, including homeworkers. Most of the regulations made under the Act apply to homeworkers as well as to employees working at an employer's workplace. These include the Management of Health and Safety at Work Regulations 1992, the Display Screen Equipment Regulations 1992, and the Provision and Use of Work Equipment Regulations 1992.

Under the Management of Health and Safety at Work Regulations 1992, employers are required to do a risk assessment of the work activities carried out by homeworkers. They need to:

- identify any hazards;
- decide who might be harmed and how;
- assess the risks and take appropriate action to remove them or reduce them as far as possible;
- record the findings; and
- check the risks from time to time and take further steps if needed.

Most teleworkers use a VDU. Under the Health and Safety (Display Screen Equipment) Regulations 1992, employers have a duty to make sure that the display screen equipment used by homeworkers is safe and does not affect the user's health.

Rather than containing detailed technical specifications or lists of approved equipment, the Regulations set more general objectives. Employers have to analyse workstations and assess and reduce risks. They should ensure that workstations meet minimum requirements; for example, screens should normally have adjustable brightness and contrast controls.

Work should be planned so there are breaks or changes of activity, depending on how intensely and for how long the employee has been using the VDU. Short frequent breaks are better than longer, less frequent ones.

If employers are requested, employers should arrange eye and eyesight tests, and provide spectacles if special ones are needed. They should also provide health and safety training to make sure employees can use all aspects of their workstation equipment safely, and know how to make best use of it to avoid health problems, for example, by adjusting the chair.

Teleworkers themselves can take precautions to ensure they get the best from their VDU equipment. They can:

• adjust the chair and VDU to find the most comfortable position – generally with arms approximately horizontal and eyes at the same height as the top of the VDU casing;

• make sure there is enough space underneath the desk to move legs freely;

• avoid excess pressure on the backs of legs and knees, possibly by using a foot-rest;

- avoid sitting in the same position for long periods;
- adjust the keyboard and screen to get a good keying and viewing position – a space in front of the keyboard may be used for resting the hands and wrists while not keying;
- avoid bending the hands up at the wrist when keying;
- try different layouts of keyboard, screen and document holder to find the best arrangement;
- ensure there is enough work space to accommodate documents;
- arrange desk and screen so that bright lights are not reflected in the screen;
- ensure the characters on the screen are sharply focused and can be read easily;
- ensure there are no layers of dirt, grime or finger marks on the screen; and
- use the brightness control on the screen to suit the lighting conditions in the room.

If homeworkers use electrical equipment provided by the employer as part of their work, the employer is responsible for its maintenance. Employers are only responsible for the equipment they supply. Electrical sockets and other parts of the homeworkers' domestic electrical system are their own responsibility.

Planning permission

In legal terms, planning permission is needed for a home office if the overall character of a dwelling will change. In practice this applies if the work is causing a nuisance or hazard to neighbours, for example if customers are visiting the premises frequently or if the work is noisy or polluting. Further details are given in the leaflet *Planning permission: a guide for business*, issued by the Department of the Environment and the Welsh Office.

Local authorities are beginning to produce their own guidelines. *Working from home – balancing the issues* is a new guide from Babergh District Council in South Suffolk. It includes a table showing under what conditions planning permission might be required when working from home. One of the examples – exclusive business use of one or more rooms or employment of staff – could affect many teleworkers. If planning permission is required, the leaflet advises that particular consideration will include:

- Could the proposals affect the quality of life of neighbours?
- Is additional traffic generated?
- Could there be an impact on road safety?
- Are the car-parking and delivery facilities adequate?
- What are the likely hours of operation? Activities outside normal working hours and at weekends are likely to be discouraged.
- Will any bulky business material need to be stored? Outside storage is unlikely to be acceptable.

Insurance

Work-related equipment and materials are often not covered in a home contents insurance policy. It is important to check the small print. Several companies have developed specific policies to cover home offices, and some insurance policies offer separate portable business equipment policies which cover the cost of re-inputting information lost if a laptop computer is stolen.

Self-employed teleworkers might consider additional health insurance, especially if they have dependants. It is possible to ensure against certain illnesses that prevent working and against the consequences of accidents. Permanent health insurance provides a regular income in the event of inability to work due to a serious injury or illness.

Professional indemnity coverage protects against work causing loss or damage to a client. Fraser (1993) reports that as yet there is no record of a library and information professional being sued on the grounds that their work caused loss or damage to their client, and that the best defence is to pay attention to professional development. However, she recommends this form of insurance to people giving advice which could result in financial loss to a client. She suggests using clear and reasonable disclaimers, like stating you have no liability for errors in published sources. For further discussion see Mowat (1998).

Data protection

If information about living individuals is held on a computer, it must be registered with the Office of the Data Protection Registrar. The standard fee is currently £75 for up to three years. The data user's register entry contains broad descriptions of the personal data which the data user holds; the purposes for which the data are used; the sources from which the data user may wish to disclose the information, as well as any overseas countries or territories to which the data user may wish to transfer the personal data.

Legal information

Self-employed teleworkers may need advice on legal aspects of running a business such as trading status and contract law. A solicitor specialising in commercial law can be found through the local public library or Chamber of Commerce. Some legal advice may be obtained from the Citizens Advice Bureau.

The Law Society administers a scheme called Lawyers For Your Business (LFYB), which represents some 1700 firms of solicitors in England and Wales. These firms have come together to help ensure that all businesses, and especially the smaller owner-managed ones, get access to sound legal advice whenever they need it. LFYB issues a series of step-by-step guides to the legal issues affecting businesses. *Contracts with customers and suppliers* discusses the problems involved in constructing a contract of business and using it, and advises on some of the issues concerning the buying of goods and services for a business.

4. Teleworking for LIS Staff

Tasks suitable for teleworking

Clearly not all kinds of work are appropriate for telework. Books need to be shelved on-site; many library users expect face-to-face contact for dealing with queries. However, when jobs are analysed, it is often found that some components may be teleworked – especially in the age of the digital library. Tasks that can be successfully carried out away from the main place of work share a number of characteristics:

- easily measurable and defined outputs;
- low need for face-to-face communication; and
- minimum physical requirements (e.g. do not require frequent access to files or bulky equipment).

The job should involve a high degree of cerebral, rather than manual, work. The work should be intrinsically satisfying, and not dependent solely on external feedback for rewards. There should be scope for a fair amount of initiative, with teleworkers given objectives and left to work with minimal supervision. Work requiring long periods of quiet concentration is particularly suited to teleworking, as is work which involves a lot of travelling.

Teleworking is more appropriate for people whose career development prospects depend as much on the development of the individual's skills as on a good knowledge of company culture.

Typical tasks for teleworking include: report writing, research, online information retrieval, editing, indexing, cataloguing, translation, computer programming, data entry, typing and word processing, and administration.

Some activities contain elements that can be teleworked. For example, although training courses for staff or users are generally delivered at a specified time and place, they may be developed off site. With increasing use of the Internet, courses are also written for distance learning. Nilles (1994) notes that, even though a worker may have a substantial requirement for face-to-face interaction, it may be possible to clump these interactions such that they all occur during one or two days of the week. This is easiest to arrange when the required face-to-face interaction is at weekly staff meetings or other regular events.

Some writers are optimistic about the potential of teleworking to provide new opportunities for LIS professionals. For instance, Lett (1994) believes that librarians of the future may well be teleworkers. She sees them as consultants, research team members, network gurus, trainers and information managers.

Telework for librarians

In a study of new patterns of work in librarianship, Pinder (1992) found only slight evidence for the development of flexible working practices (she looked at teleworking alongside job-sharing and flexible working time). The most developed was job-sharing, which was practised in some public libraries through encouragement by local authorities. Flexible working time was better developed in polytechnic libraries than in university or public libraries. Teleworking, she found, was virtually unheard of in public libraries.

In a survey of 60 American libraries, 12% were found to have employees who regularly worked at home (Heinz 1990). This was more common in academic libraries (24% of those using homeworkers) than in public libraries (12%). At Boulder Public Library, teleworking managers were reported to spend one day a week at home (Luce & Hartman 1984).

Pinder believes that flexible working is particularly relevant for libraries, in which a high proportion of the workforce are women, whose skills are often lost when they leave the profession to raise a family. She argues that, if libraries are to compete for scarce skills in a tight labour market, they must begin to adopt more flexible patterns of work. A similar case is made by Lett (1993), who notes that demographic trends within the workforce are moving organisations towards more flexible structures. Lett also points out that those areas of the library world which are information focused with staff in

IT are fertile ground for teleworking. She envisages LIS workers at the forefront of shaping new forms of organisation.

The Library Association has taken up the challenge to inform its members about teleworking by publishing material on the subject. Its leaflet *Teleworking*, which is intended as a starting point, is concerned with those wishing to work for an employer under permanent conditions of employment. It provides information for employees on expertise, ways of working, isolation and professional development. A checklist for employers covers such issues as equipment and supplies, conditions of work, security of data, staff management and recruitment. *Working for yourself* is a Library Association brochure aimed at self-employed workers in the library and information world (Fraser 1993). It offers sensible advice on topics ranging from working from home, through marketing, to financial considerations.

An article in the *LA Record* gives an interesting account of the teleworking experiences of a member of the senior management team from Somerset's Library Service (Campbell and Froud 1995). When Jacquie Campbell first became a mother, she approached the County Council's Personnel Department about the possibility of teleworking. After examining her job, the Personnel Department was supportive. Much of her work involved preparing written reports and papers, dealing with correspondence and internal communications and planning new services and projects; in addition, she spent a significant amount of time on the telephone.

It was established that, with the appropriate equipment, this work could be carried out anywhere.

On her return to work, Campbell worked at home for two days a week. She organised her work so that paperwork and most telephoning were carried out during teleworking days, with meetings and visits scheduled for the other days. Her line manager, Rob Froud (then Deputy County Librarian), gave his point of view. He made the point that, 'Many senior public librarians may wonder whether they can afford to release staff to work at home for even part of their time. As telecommunications become less expensive, as issues of recruitment and retention become significant, and as environmental issues around travel to work gain ground perhaps they should ask whether they can afford *not* to look at it seriously with staff who want to take this option. Certainly the experience in Somerset is that a committed, organised and energetic member of the senior management team will repay the small investment with dividends.'

Consultancy

A number of LIS professionals work as information consultants of one sort or another. They include part-timers such as university staff as well as retired people who want to keep in touch with the field and their former colleagues and perhaps supplement their pension.

Some consultants set out to start and grow a business, while others prefer to work independently, juggling the demands of changing amounts of work. Others form partnerships or participate with colleagues as members of consortia.

One definition of a consultant is 'a specialist who gives expert advice on information' (LA/IIS guidelines for consultants working in librarianship and information science 1983). Such activity may include:

- advising a client on matters within the expertise of the consultant;
- developing new skills or knowledge on behalf of a client;
- reviewing and evaluating technologies on behalf of a client; or
- performing specific professional tasks based on a consultant's specialist knowledge, including staff selection, education and development.

Information consultancy grew out of the library sector and expanded when library automation systems became widespread. Consultants were able to provide advice to librarians who had little experience of computers. When John Ashford formed his consultancy in 1974, most of the projects he dealt with were concerned with library automation (Ashford, 1985). He noted that the focus shifted first to storage and retrieval of textual material in online systems, and then more and more to the computer-assisted management of very large document collections.

Other activities consultants may be involved in are information audits, database design, records management, literature surveys, online searching, training, marketing and recruitment. Some information consultants produce information products like journals, books, reference sources or software packages. Nowadays consultants' expertise includes the Internet, intranets and electronic commerce.

O'Leary (1987) uses the term information broker to refer to an independent information professional. However, he points out that some people like to distinguish between an information broker (someone who looks up information for you) and an information consultant (who tells you what to do with the information and how to do it). He considers that, in its broadest usage, consultant can also refer to library services like cataloguing and collection development, and to editorial services like indexing, abstracting and writing.

Gurnsey and White (1989) are keen to distinguish between consultants and freelance workers in the LIS field, such as freelance librarians and researchers. For them, 'consultancy does not mean the mere performance of a task, it means a degree of advice concerning change based upon proven expertise and experience. It is a function typically performed at a senior or policy level and few *true* consultants can expect to be working at a junior level' (p. 5).

From a teleworking perspective, whether one performs a task or gives advice or whether one works at a senior or junior level is less significant than employment status. A self-employed worker needs a number of characteristics, the most important of which is good health. Qualities that are desirable in consultants include imagination, self-confidence, impartiality and analytical ability. Consultants need

45

to be able to sell their skills, organise their finances and develop their expertise. They need enough resources to set up the business and keep going not just until work has been commissioned but through the work process and until payment has been made. Family support is essential.

To Finer (1984) the ideal consultant 'is intelligent, emotionally mature, empathetic, personable, has integrity, an independent and objective spirit, self-confidence, a basic orientation to people, is good at planning, and is skilled in expression and training. He or she has a wide theoretical and practical understanding of all aspects of library and information systems, is perhaps a specialist in one particular area of the field, and also has a knowledge of organisation theory, group psychology and the change process.'

Vickers (1990) places importance on the personality of consultants, and stresses that they must be able to communicate and work with people at all levels. 'They should have a pleasant temperament that encourages people to speak openly to them, yet be able to show firmness when necessary. Technical competence is of little use on its own, without the right personal qualities.'

While it is generally recommended that information consultants should have considerable experience as practising information specialists, some library schools are introducing the subject to their students. Kehoe (1997) believes that LIS programmes should provide students with education and training for information broking in preparation for a career in this field. She recommends that relevant courses should focus on small business management (especially marketing and accounting) and research skills. The latter go beyond online searching, and encompass analysis, evaluation and writing skills. Kehoe points out that research and reference skills are not equivalent, and observes that, whereas an online searcher in an academic library may simply hand over the entire transcript of a search to a patron, a broker must be able to add value to the search: the broker ensures that the presentation looks professional and includes an interpretation of the information provided.

It is a paradox that self-employment can provide a lifestyle of freedom and flexibility but it also involves organisational responsibilities way beyond those expected of most employees. The failure of an information business is more likely to result from a shortage of business skills than because of a shortage of expertise (O'Leary 1987). Genaway (1992) notes that, while independence is a common motive for becoming a consultant, it is ironic because one becomes totally reliant on clients, on establishing and building a clientele, and always planning for the next job while working on the current one.

5. Case Studies

This chapter provides examples of teleworking among library and information workers. The aim is to present 'snapshots' to show the reality and diversity of teleworking in action. Many of the case studies were obtained in response to a request on the listserv LIS-LINK. Some teleworkers have written their own accounts. Others were put together via personal, telephone or email interviews – with email follow-ups to check accuracy. There are more accounts of self-employed professionals than those employed in libraries, but this probably reflects the current situation in the UK. In addition to librarians and consultants, some case studies describe situations where teleworking is carried out for only part of the time.

Teleworkers in library settings

University of London Library: teleworking trial from the Library's viewpoint

As part of the Goldsmiths' Library of Economic Literature Catalogue Retro-conversion Project, the University of London Library has been faced with the need to edit a large number of catalogue records in a limited period, at a time when for various reasons, workspace for staff was at a premium. Teleworking became an attractive option in these circumstances, although it was a completely new venture for the Library. A suitable candidate was found, with experience of cataloguing and histori-

49

cal bibliography, and with the necessary computer equipment already installed at home. A trial three-month contract was drawn up, with the intention of establishing a clear framework for both sides, with agreed targets. The teleworker spent two days in the Library at the beginning of the contract, for training and general familiarisation, and continues to work in the Library for three hours a week. This enables cards to be returned and collected, and queries to be resolved, and is useful in maintaining personal contact and including the teleworker as part of the project team.

Costs associated with setting up the arrangement

- Transit boxes for the catalogue cards.
- Instruction manuals.
- Cataloguing manuals and support documentation.
- Basic stationery.
- Library staff time spent on intensive training.

Advantages

- Relieving pressures on, and costs of providing, staff working space in the Library.
- Saving in the costs of overheads for a member of staff.
- Saving on expenses of providing computer equipment.
- Testing remote communications to the Library system: for example, we are making interesting discoveries about system response times at different times of day.

Disadvantages

• Lack of immediate communication, especially when serious cataloguing problems arise.

Potential problems

• Insurance cover for use of the computer equipment for business purposes – we have held this to be the responsibility of the teleworker.

• Ensuring time spent connected to the system is used purely for editing or associated use of the system.

• Security of cards in transit between the Library and the worker's home site.

• Negotiating with teleworker on using cheap-rate time to connect to the Library.

• Clarifying how the assessment of record throughput will be calculated: that is, if the number of records per hour is calculated on the time spent cataloguing from home, it is higher than if the calculation includes the time spent in the Library each week. This is an aspect we are considering at the moment.

General assessment

Thus far the experiment is proving beneficial to the Library, both financially and in practical terms. The teleworker is making a significant contribution to the cataloguing throughput, and it is anticipated that this will continue to rise as her expertise increases. The whole arrangement has to be based on a certain amount of mutual trust. We were fortunate to find a candidate whose home equipment was (almost) immediately compatible with our system. It would not have been so much to the Library's benefit if we had had to provide equipment for the teleworker, although I can envisage circumstances when this might be necessary.

University of London Library: teleworking trial from the teleworker's viewpoint

I am the teleworker on the Goldsmiths' Library of Economic Literature Catalogue Retroconversion Project at the University of London Library. All comments refer to my situation as the teleworker, not to the Library. The work involves checking the entries on a computerised catalogue against the original card-based catalogue and editing the entries. I currently have a three-month contract with the University Library, under which I agree to work a minimum of 13 and a maximum of 15 hours per week. Three of these hours are worked on the Library's premises; the rest of the time I am working from home, using my own PC. I access the computer catalogue via my ISP (Virgin Net in this case), using a telnet address supplied by the Library.

Advantages

I am able to work at any time of the day, as the computer catalogue is always available, unless work is being carried out on the system. There are no distractions from other workers, or demands upon me to undertake any other duties. This means that I am able to concentrate on the task in hand. I am working in my home environment, and it's up to me when I stop for breaks, meals, and so on (and it's comfortable here). Going into the Library every week gives me a chance to feel part of the project team and to talk over problems with others doing the same kind of work.

Disadvantages

Getting a response to any queries may have to wait longer than if I were on site all the time. If the system goes down for any reason, and I'm not told, it can be frustrating. It also means I'm going to drop behind in my input and this may affect my income. There would be a similar problem if my own PC went down for any reason, as I have no alternative machine. I can feel a bit isolated sometimes!

Overall comments

I understand that the Library is pleased with the results of this experiment, so far. I am certainly happy with the work, which I find interesting. However, I believe there are two reasons for the success of this particular project: I'm used to working on my own, anyway, and I live within walking distance of the Library, so it's easy to take the catalogue cards backwards and forwards. Cataloguing is an area which certainly offers opportunities for teleworking and seems, in this case, to have thrown up very few problems, and none that have proved insoluble. The project continues to be experimental, and will be re-assessed at a later date.

Somerset Library Service

The article mentioned above in Chapter 4 (Campbell & Froud 1995) is an excellent introduction for librarians thinking of teleworking and for their managers. It covers the teleworker's experience of working space, scheduling, working methods, communications, monitoring, finance, benefits and problems, and summarises the key issues. The manager then adds his comments.

Self-employed LIS professionals

Phil Bradley

Phil Bradley is an Internet consultant, trainer, web designer and author. Following an honours degree in librarianship, he worked for the British Council as an information professional, then with SilverPlatter – first in technical support, then as director of training, and finally as web master. He made a definite decision to become a teleworker: 'I couldn't stand working in a 9-5 job any longer and wanted to change the entire way in which I worked. I wanted to control my own hours and work when I pleased.'

Phil works mainly at home – on activities like web page design and writing – but also travels to various organisations to provide on-site training sessions. A lot of his work is carried out via email: 'This works well for me. It is very useful to have things in print from clients. They have to think about what they want to do. On the phone, frequently no specific conclusions are reached.' Collaboration on the

Know How Guide *World Wide Web: How to design and construct home pages,* which he co-authored with Anna Smith, was entirely by email. Working online so much of the time makes a second phone line essential.

Phil's own web site (http://www.philb.com) is of crucial importance in his work: 'I couldn't do without the web site. It is integral to all I do.' Not only is it a source of information about himself and his work for potential clients, but he makes active use of it – for example, when creating a website for a client, he can provide samples of possible ways of presenting the information on his own site, which the client can then access. All his articles are on the Internet and when he travels on business he is able to retrieve his notes from his website.

As a teleworker, Phil feels he works more effectively and achieves higher productivity. With more flexibility to choose his hours of work, he finds he can get a lot done between midnight and 4.00 am. He estimates he does as much work in three to four hours at home as he would in a whole day in an office, because there are no interruptions at home. Another bonus is not having to commute, which gives him an extra two to three hours a day.

He has the flexibility to choose between work and the garden; it is easy to leave work completely for a while. That said, he stresses the importance of an understanding partner: 'Jill takes the view that, although I'm at home, I'm also at work, so she doesn't expect me to take time out to wash the dishes and have supper ready for her either. (Though it has to be said that I often do both!) I think it could be really difficult if you had a partner who thought that just because you worked at home, it also meant that by default you would do "home type things" as well.'

He appreciates being able to work how he wants to. Describing himself as an untidy person, he finds he can work well with piles of papers everywhere. At home there is no one telling him to tidy up because of visitors. He is glad to have his own office.

On the downside, Phil finds that teleworking can be lonely without face-to-face interaction. He misses gossip and the chatter round the coffee machine. To counteract this, he uses Internet relay chat quite heavily.

Phil does not feel professional isolation. He knows which websites are useful to look at and spends two days a week on the Internet to keep up. In addition, he uses mailing lists, subscribes to a small number of journals, and attends conferences and exhibitions. He gains contact and feedback through the courses he runs, and learns from the delegates.

In the two and a half years he has worked independently, Phil has never regretted leaving full-time employment. However, he says he would find it difficult to work on the Shetland Islands. 'Teleworking for 80% of the time is fine, but it is important to live within about an hour's reach of London. At the moment I feel very lucky.'

Lynne Clitheroe

Lynne Clitheroe has been a teleworker since March 1998. Before setting up and managing an enquiry service in London for three years, Lynne was an Information Specialist at the University of Warwick Business Information Service.

A number of people encouraged Lynne to go freelance. She found there was a niche in the market for a specialised service providing statistical information to large companies. Deciding to set up on her own, she established a rapid response enquiry service. In addition to answering enquiries on such subjects as economic trends, forecasts and business and finance, she provides in-house training courses on topics like recent developments in published statistics, sources of economic and business statistics, and understanding economic indicators.

Despite working on her own, Lynne does not lack professional contact. As she lives near the Export Market Information Centre (EMIC), she often uses its resources to respond to queries, and has good contacts with the staff there as well as those in other information centres. She is on friendly terms with clients and keeps in touch on a business and social level, using, for example, networking opportunities like the City Information Group. She is glad to be based in London so that she can attend meetings.

Lynne spends a lot of time on the phone and therefore does not get lonely. Although she gets some enquiries by email, most are initially by phone and are followed up by fax or email. Because the information she provides is highly statistical and is difficult to send by email, she delivers completed assignments by post, courier (most clients are in London) or fax.

For Lynne, the biggest benefit of teleworking is the freedom. While the nature of the work is very similar to what she was doing in her previous jobs, she is now free to decide how to handle specific enquiries without interference from others. In addition, most of the money her clients pay out goes directly to her and the quality of her life has changed enormously for the better.

Running an enquiry service, she does not know in advance whether she will have work for the day or not. When she was employed from nine to five, she had to fill in time when there was no work. At home she can do something else. This uncertainty also represents a downside. Although she does not panic if there is no work, she misses the challenge when it is not there as she gets considerable intellectual satisfaction from it.

Lynne has not yet started fully marketing her services. Because the need for statistics can be erratic, she needs to work on the basis of attracting a lot of clients and is prepared to work long hours if the demand is there.

Looking to the future, Lynne is interested in how the Internet may affect work. Some clients pay her to search the Internet, but many of the statistics she provides are difficult to obtain or understand, and are not available, or reliable enough, on the Internet. She feels a flexible approach is necessary.

Dr Justus Krabshuis

Dr Justus Krabshuis has been a teleworker since the mid-1970s, when he went to live in the Scottish Highlands and needed to find a way to support himself. With a doctorate in Sociology and Anthropology, he set about making use of his academic background. By writing to publishers offering translation and editorial skills, he obtained work from Elsevier Publishing in Amsterdam. Starting from translating and indexing for the medical database, Embase, he developed expertise in online information for medicine and health. This led to further assignments – partly from other clients and partly developing his role within Elsevier to include Embase training.

He went on to establish Highland Data, a small business providing information brokerage, electronic publishing consultancy and online training services, as well as current awareness and alerting services to industry.

For Justus, teleworking provides an opportunity to earn a living in a beautiful part of Scotland where there are few employment opportunities. He is based some two and a half hours drive out of Glasgow. Being so far from major cities is occasionally a drawback; however, he travels frequently in Europe and flights are only slightly longer from Glasgow than from other UK cities. High expenditure on travel is one of his overheads.

Justus has been involved with teleworking initiatives in Scotland for a number of years, and is now somewhat sceptical about its potential to improve the employment situation in the Highlands. He deplores the lack of business acumen among many self-employed teleworkers and stresses the necessity of being able to sell skills to clients and to develop new skills for which there is a market.

Nonetheless, he would like to be able to help library and information professionals set up in remote parts of Scotland, and has expressed willingness to respond to people's emails if they have questions or would like some 'discussion' and/or help in setting up their own operation. He can be contacted on 73064.1412@compuserve.com.

Alison Scammell

Since preparing this case study Alison has been appointed as a commissioning editor for Aslib Publications. She says that the experience described below will make a considerable contribution to this role and to her general career development.

I have a background in special librarianship having spent seven years managing the information service at a large trade association. I entered the LIS profession quite late after getting a degree in English and History and I did a range of different jobs before completing the postgraduate DipLib at the Polytechnic of North London in 1986.

I left work in 1994 to have a family (my twins are now four years old) and even before I started maternity leave I had decided that I wanted to pursue a freelance career at least for the time being. I felt there was little scope for further promotion in my organisation and had always liked the idea of working for myself. While I was pregnant I had started a Masters degree (in information and communication studies) at the University of North London and was able to complete the degree a year later.

I became self-employed and worked as an independent Information Management Consultant. Like most consultants in this field I had a portfolio of different freelance activities including research, writing, speaking and training. I was totally responsible for earning my own income, providing my own equipment and office facilities and for finding new business. I often worked with other consultants and was always looking to establish new contacts and partnerships. Networking (both physically and electronically) took up a considerable part of my time, but was one of the most enjoyable aspects of my business. I am currently researching for a part-time PhD (at City University) which fitted in very well with my work as it kept me at the cutting edge of developments in my field. I was also the advertising Account Director for an Internet newsletter called *Free Pint* (again entirely on a self-employed, commission-earning basis).

The work I did on *Free Pint* was interesting because this was an innovative and exciting publishing venture and I was part of a virtual organisation. There were three of us in the organisation and we communicated almost entirely by email and phone. The work provided an opportunity to be part of a close-knit team and I enjoyed interacting with colleagues instead of working entirely in a solitary capacity. It also allowed me to extend my network of contacts in the profession and the publishing/information provider sector.

One area of my work was something I have called 'door-to-door' Internet training and advice. I found that there was great demand for 'ordinary' people to learn about the Internet on a one-to-one basis, in their own homes. I took my laptop to clients and tailored training to meet their specific needs. Although I invested in advertising (in local papers and newsletters), I also found new clients by word of mouth and personal recommendation. To me, being a teleworker was about being able to work in a flexible, location-independent way, optimising the benefits of technology and taking an entrepreneurial approach to information provision. It also meant getting out and about, meeting clients and colleagues and keeping up with industry developments. These are now proving useful in my new job.

There were several reasons for becoming a teleworker at that time. Like a lot of women, I wanted to be able to find fulfilling and reasonably paid work which could fit in well with the demands of family life. Teleworking parents still do need to ensure they have adequate childcare arrangements but it has allowed me to spend more time with the children. There are also disadvantages of course. It can be hard to concentrate when the children make a lot of noise and there are other distractions around the house. You need to be extremely self-motivated and disciplined, and have good time management skills.

Apart from the general flexibility of the work and the ability to spend a lot of time with the children, the main benefit of teleworking for me has been that it allowed me to do a range of different jobs. The constant challenge was in keeping up with developments in such a fast changing field and I had to be responsible for my own training in order to acquire new skills. One disadvantage is that the rest of the world can sometimes seem slow to adapt to new ways of location-independent work. I would like to be able to access more (non-Internet) library and information facilities, for my research. For example, although I am able to use some online services at the university, it is not possible to access these from home. I don't think enough is being done to provide library and information services to remote workers, and I am currently researching these (and other information needs issues), for my PhD.

I have other long-term career ambitions but I hope to retain many aspects of teleworking throughout my entire career.

Part-time teleworking

Juliet Amissah

Juliet Amissah became a teleworker while taking a postgraduate course on electronic publishing in the Department of Information Science at City University. In addition to editorial work on a newsletter, she is engaged on a project creating a website for a newspaper in Ghana.

Although the project is temporary, Juliet enjoys teleworking and would like to work from home in the future. She appreciates being able to get on with work at her own pace without being disturbed, and is glad not to be involved in office politics.

The main problem is waiting for feedback. The newspaper in Ghana tends to take a long time responding to her queries and providing a reaction to the work she has completed. She needs the feedback to know how to continue with the assignment.

The only other drawback of working from home is that it is sometimes difficult to work when the weather is warm and sunny. However, Juliet feels this is far outweighed by the increased productivity at other times.

Juliet has no feelings of isolation working on her own. Although she would be interested to visit the office, she does not consider it necessary to carry out her work effectively.

Nicola Harrison

Nicola Harrison is a Project Assistant for the Edinburgh Engineering Virtual Library (EEVL) based at Heriot Watt University – working 14 hours a week at home, and one morning a week (three hours) in the Heriot Watt Library. In addition, for three hours a week, she works as a technical writer for Derwent Information. She writes:

Following a degree in Electrical and Electronic Engineering, I worked as an engineer for 18 months, then became a technical writer and coder at Derwent Information for three and a half years.

The coding part of the job involved applying an alphanumeric classification describing novel features of inventions. I specialised in classifying computer peripherals, photocopiers and faxes, and medical electronics.

When I married, my husband initially moved to London where I worked, because I was earning more, but, after six months, we decided to move to Edinburgh, where he came from, because it was a nicer environment. The only job I could find was as a Civil Service filing clerk, on approximately a third of my previous salary. I started teleworking (10 hours a week) for Derwent, partly to keep my technical knowledge up to date, and partly to supplement my low income. I left my job with the Civil Service after a year when my first child was born, and continued with the telework technical writing (16 hours a week) from when she was six weeks old.

In my work at EEVL, I review engineering-related Internet sites and determine whether they have sufficient useful information on them to be worth adding to the EEVL database. I check reviews of sites provided by volunteers in several other University Libraries. I also check the integrity of links from EEVL to the sites listed, correct errors, and update records.

I have also continued with the technical writing for three hours a week, since the Project Assistant job is only funded for six months at a time, and I don't know how long it will last. I review patent documents and produce abstracts of them as well as lists of their uses and particular advantages.

The major advantage of teleworking is that I'm able to be at home with my children almost all the time. I can adjust my work schedule to fit around their activities, illnesses, etc. When they were babies I set a rocker chair up beside my desk and operated it with my foot while I typed. I also used to read documents out loud while I worked, which the children seemed to like, until they got old enough to understand the words. Now they are two and three years old they are happy to play together most of the time. Sometimes they sit on my lap while I work. They have a toy typewriter which they use to imitate me at work. They also like sitting beside me and drawing pictures.

I don't have to travel to work every day, which saves on busfares as well as travelling time, and also makes me feel that I'm not adding to the problem of global warming. I save on childcare expenses. With two children, nursery fees would account for around half of my salary. I also avoid the worries of finding a good nursery where my children would be safe and happy. Ideally, I would like to continue teleworking until my children have finished at primary school, so that I can be at home when they return from school.

Disadvantages include missing meetings when they don't coincide with the time when I'm in the office. I also miss out on some of the informal discussions which can develop in the workplace, although I do communicate with my colleagues several times a day via email.

It can be very hard work managing children and a job at the same time. I try to work in short bursts and give the children attention when they need it, even if this means breaking off in the middle of something. Unfortunately this sometimes results in me doing my work after midnight to make up for lost time. My children also see more television than I would like. I often put a video on for them in order to get some time to catch up with work. My older child is at playgroup in the mornings, and after the summer the younger one will go too. This will give me two and a half hours every morning without interruptions, which should make my working life much easier. Another disadvantage of the teleworking is that if I end up working in the evening very often my husband feels neglected. This has been less of a problem since he got his own computer and began playing computer games.

I am an employee of EEVL, but self employed in my work for Derwent Information. I own my computer, desk, etc and insure them myself. I pay the Internet subscription fee of £10 per month, but my employer pays the phone bill of over £200 a quarter. Since my EEVL work is all related to the Internet, the location I work from makes no difference at all.

Peter Williams

Part of Peter Williams' employment is teleworking for the web edition of the *Northern Echo*, which has its headquarters in Darlington. This work contributes to research he is doing on journalists and the Internet in the Department of Information Science at City University. He is also involved in university work like teaching, writing and editing, as well as research on his PhD.

There are two aspects to his work on the *Northern Echo:* research and evaluation of websites; and providing an electronic reference service from the newspaper's background stories (for example, in the areas of community, recreation and leisure). During the World Cup, one of his tasks is to take material from World Cup sites on the Internet and repackage them for the newspaper with commentary on content and technology.

Email is Peter's preferred means of contact with the *Northern Echo* for routine matters. He has an incurable dislike of bothering people on the phone at work – despite the fact that journalists do much of their work over the phone – although he is happy to receive calls. This can delay matters, as his Darlington colleagues tend to check their email less often than Peter and his academic friends might. Several times a month he visits Darlington to attend an editorial conference.

Peter's employment situation is complicated. He has been employed by the university on a fixed-term contract based on external funding (from the British Library). The *Northern Echo* opportunity arrived just as this funding ran out, giving him a lifeline until funding from the same source becomes forthcoming for the second stage of the British Library project.

Apart from the advantages to Peter of a job and – a bonus – continuous employment with the university, the setup is beneficial to the university itself in that the department is interested in the Internet and the news media, and through Peter can get access to staff on the paper and can collect useful data. This includes details of Internet logs on the newspaper's web site as well as good knowledge of news sites. The newspaper benefits by not having to pay overheads.

Working from a remote location, Peter finds he is better able to concentrate on the job in hand. On site he would be roped into other work. He sees teleworking as a way of getting the job done without getting sucked into extraneous activities. Technically there is no problem doing the work at a distance from the newspaper.

However, there are fewer opportunities for exchanging ideas, such as deciding the relative importance of certain news stories from the paper's point of view, and for discussing issues of layout and design (Peter is not an expert at HTML and would like to benefit more from the experience of others).

6. Information for Teleworking

Increasing changes in ways of working and technological possibilities point to the need for up-to-date information. Huws (1997) notes the importance of the provision of information in the facilitation of teleworking.

Kinds of information

The information needs of teleworkers are influenced by the nature of their work and by their employment status. Beyond that is information needed to create an environment for teleworking (Blake 1995, Blake *et al.* 1996), a need most evident in self-employed teleworkers and those based at home.

Much of the information needed by teleworkers will depend on their profession, and will be obtained via means common to that profession, such as membership of professional bodies, subscriptions to specialist periodicals and networking.

A membership survey by the Telework Telecottage and Telecentre Association (TCA, an organisation for teleworkers) indicated needs for information on technology, individual teleworking arrangements and obtaining work. Huws suggests that existing teleworkers require information about safe working practices, employment rights, sources of advice and training opportunities.

Teleworkers in full employment may expect to receive much of their information directly from their own organisation. Reporting on the information needs of teleworkers in the retail financial sector, Scammell (1995) found a marked reliance on 'value added' information from this source.

The information needs of self-employed teleworkers are similar to those of small businesses. These teleworkers need to be aware of information related to their self-employed status – such as legislation, marketing, insurance, finance – and they need information to help them to buy, maintain and upgrade their computer and telecommunications equipment. Surveys carried out by the National Union of Journalists indicate that freelance journalists have needs quite distinct from those of staff journalists (Huws, 1997). These include advice on tax, copyright and the negotiation of contracts and a need for training.

Employers need information on the setting up and management of teleworking schemes including technical information, information about legal, contractual, planning, insurance and related issues, information about sources of advice and consultancy, and information about good employment practice (Huws 1997).

Other groups requiring information about teleworking are training agencies and the unemployed. Training agencies need to know about the skill requirements of teleworking, while unemployed people require information about new work and training opportunities.

Role of libraries

Library and information centres in organisations that employ teleworkers have an important role to play in providing information to those people who work remotely. Not only do they provide information directly to individual teleworkers, but they are in an ideal position to ensure that the corporate intranet is kept up to date and that it contains the information needed for teleworkers to do their jobs effectively. Special libraries responsible for knowledge management strategy within an organisation need to be aware of the contribution that teleworkers can make.

Public libraries represent one of the greatest educational, cultural and social resources in Britain (Comedia 1993). With over four thousand service points in the UK, they have enormous potential as providers of information to teleworkers throughout the country. As well as being able to offer business information to self-employed teleworkers, they are well-positioned to provide some help with IT.

Increasingly, public libraries are making information technology available to users. In 1997, 85% of 191 public library authorities in the UK provided CD-ROM facilities for public use and 46% reported the provision of public access to the Internet (Batt 1998). However, there is a contrast between the high numbers of authorities providing public access to IT resources and the low number of service points at which those applications are provided; 74% of library authorities have the Internet, but only 5% of service points in the UK offer public access.

Various reports highlight the importance of information technology for the development of public library services in the future. For example, the DNH Review of the Public Library Service in England and Wales (Aslib 1995) notes the appeal of public libraries to homeworkers and business people who run small enterprises, and suggests such people are more at ease in a public library than in Chambers of Commerce, Business Links or other formal services. The authors found that individuals who worked from home or teleworked were the most intensive users of all who visited public libraries.

A report from the Library and Information Commission *(New library: the people's network)* recommends establishing a development agency – the Public Library Networking Agency – to energise and coordinate UK-wide networking developments. This agency should be charged with developing the public library network through the creation of a UK 'backbone' infrastructure to link individual public library networks, and negotiation with library authorities to upgrade local library networks to a common UK standard on a shared-funding basis. The authors have a vision of the public library as the natural place for people to turn to for advice, support and practical training in IT and common skills. They suggest it could potentially play a significant role in training and retraining.

Not only can public libraries serve as an IT resource, they are increasingly taking on the role of IT learning resource. Of 140 library authorities, 40 offer user training – many in collaboration with an FE college or Input/Output centre. Run by a private company, Input/Output centres manage public access computer centres within libraries. These centres offer a range of services including computer hire, computer application training and Internet access. The public library is at the heart of the National Grid for Learning.

Gray *et al*. (1993) report that libraries are ideal telecentres. A few years ago, the DNH Public Library Review (Aslib 1995) recommended that telecentre facilities should be developed in public libraries. This idea is being realised in some libraries: Batt reports 59 authorities with telecentres installed and running or planned for the near future. Huyton Library, for instance, has a telecentre with over 30 PCs available for public use.

Tomos (1997) writes of successful telecentre ventures in Wales, where telecentres are becoming community centres as well as encompassing a more traditional support role for teleworkers. She believes there is an important opportunity for public library services to develop facilities and staff skills to service this growing sector, and laments the fact that few library services have offered their services (p 19). 'If telecentres become the local node for collaborative public information networks and scarce resources are prioritized in their direction, the imperative is greater for library services to examine the possibility of developing premises and staff capabilities to take advantage of the opportunity.'

Some observers are concerned about the longer-term implications of an increase in teleworking for LIS professionals in relation to the disintermediation debate. A key aspect of teleworking is the empowerment of individuals, which means they are becoming responsible for their own information needs. Unisys, which has a high proportion of flexible workers, is radically re-inventing its organisational structures. The company has dispensed with its library and information function altogether; instead they are building their information infrastructure around high tech business centres and an intranet.

The importance of public libraries to teleworkers will depend on how libraries develop and the role they will come to play within the community. Dempsey's (1997) vision of the types of services that public libraries of the future might provide include many that would interest teleworkers – electronic reference rooms based on shared access to encyclopaedia and dictionary resources; improved systems for unified access to diverse bibliographic information resources, business intelligence services, civic and government information resources; and online mentoring.

Stonier (1990) draws attention to the physical nature of the future public library. He views it as a place for homeworkers to go when they need an excuse to go out and socialise. He considers libraries should create attractive coffee shops and wine bars. They should include facilities for desktop publishing and studios for producing sound and videotape. They should evolve into information hypermarkets with bookshops, record shops, computer shops, film theatres and museums. Then they would expand the vital social role for which they were created: to strengthen the cultural and intellectual life of the communities they serve.

7. The Teleworking Culture: Conclusions

This guide has provided a brief introduction to basic aspects of teleworking and indicated how teleworking may be of benefit to LIS professionals. While teleworking may not always be appropriate, it can be very effective in certain situations. For example, it can contribute to the retention of skilled staff and result in improved productivity. With reduced commuting and more personal flexibility, it can enhance the quality of life for individual teleworkers. On the down side, some managers find teleworking difficult to manage, and some teleworkers suffer from isolation.

Successful teleworking requires good management skills and an awareness of the issues involved. These include identifying jobs suitable for teleworking and selecting suitable people. Guidelines are useful to clarify the responsibilities of teleworkers and their managers. Generally they cover issues like ownership of equipment and arrangements regarding its repair, payment of bills for heating and telecommunications, insurance of work and equipment, health and safety, and training.

Effective communication is crucial to successful teleworking, along with the ability to select appropriate technology for particular kinds of communication. Training should be provided both for teleworkers and their managers.

For home-based teleworking, adequate space is necessary for working and storage. Security arrangements should be in place to protect both work and equipment. Issues to be considered include health and safety legislation; planning permission; insurance; and data protection legislation.

Tasks that are suitable for teleworking should have easily measurable and defined outputs, a low need for face-to-face communication, and minimum physical requirements. In a library or information service environment, typical tasks for teleworking include report writing, research, online information retrieval and cataloguing. While teleworking is still fairly uncommon among library staff, many LIS professionals work as information consultants. Libraries are well placed to provide information to teleworkers.

As libraries and information centres develop, and take on board new methods of working and new IT-based services, there are opportunities for LIS professionals to review their services and procedures to see whether any of these could be better served by the employment of teleworkers, on either a short-term or permanent basis. Some of these will as yet be unthought of, but experience to date suggests a wealth of exciting possibilities ahead.

8. Further Reading

Apgar, M (1998). 'The alternative workplace: changing where and how people work.' *Harvard Business Review* May-June, pp. 121-136.

Ashford, J H (1985). 'Application in practice of the results of library and information retrieval research – experience in consultancy.' *Journal of Information Science* 10 (1), pp. 11-16.

Aslib (1995). *Review of the public library service in England and Wales for the Department of National Heritage: final report.* London: Aslib.

Batt, C (1998). *Information technology in public libraries*, 6th edition. London: Library Association Publishing.

Bertin, I & Denbigh, A (1998). *The teleworking handbook: new ways of working in the information society*, 2nd edition. Kenilworth: Telework Telecottage and Telecentre Association (TCA).

Blake, M (1995). *Information for teleworkers*. (British Library R&D Report 6199). London: British Library.

Blake, M, Creek, J & Haynes, D (1996). *Teleworking – a guide to sources of information*. (British Library R&D Report 6226). London: British Library.

Blake, M, Cookman, N & Haynes, D (1999). *Teleworking directory*. London: British Library Science Reference Information Service.

Blaxter, T (1995). 'Managing teleworkers: the Crossaig experience.' *Managing Information* 2 (5), pp. 30- 32.

Campbell, J & Froud, R (1995). 'Teleworking works!' *Library Association Record* 87 (12), pp. 654-657.

Comedia (1993). *Borrowed time: the future of public libraries in the UK.* Bowines Green: Comedia.

Currin, K & Williams, G (1997). *Manual of remote working.* Aldershot: Gower.

Davenport, E & Wormell, I (1997). 'Telework 96: an international collaborative learning package for information entrepreneurs.' *Education for Information* 15, pp. 43-56.

Dempsey, L (1997). 'Public libraries and networking: some introductory remarks. In *The Internet, networking and the public library* (ed. S. Ormes & L. Dempsey), London: Library Association Publishing/UKOLN, pp XI-XIII.

European Commission (1998). *Telework 98: status report on European telework.* Brussels: European Commission DG XIII-B.

Finer, R (1984). *The role of consultants in information management.* Bradford: MCB University Press.

Fraser, V (1993). *Working for yourself.* London: The Library Association.

Genaway, D C (1992). 'What makes a consultant a consultant?' In *Using consultants in libraries and information centres: a management handbook* (ed. E D Garten), Westport: Greenwood Press, 29-37.

Gray, M, Hodson, N & Gordon, G (1993). *Teleworking explained.* Chichester: John Wiley & Sons.

Gurnsey, J & White, M S (1989). *Information consultancy.* London: Clive Bingley.

Handy, C (1990). *The age of unreason*. London: Arrow.

Heinz, M (1990). 'Taking work home.' *Library Personnel News* 4 Winter 2 (cited by Pinder, 1992).

Huws, U (1996). *Teleworking: an overview of the research*, London: Analytica.

Huws, U (1997). *Teleworking: guidelines for good practice*. Brighton: The Institute for Employment Studies.

Kehoe, C A (1997). Educating information brokers. *Journal of Education for Library and Information Science* 38 (1). Winter, pp. 66-70.

Kinsman, F (1987). *The telecommuters*. Chichester: John Wiley.

Kinsman, F (1991). *Millenium: towards tomorrow's society*. London: Penguin.

Korte, W B & Wynne, R (1996). *Telework: penetration, potential and practice in Europe*. Amsterdam: IOS Press.

Leaman, A & Borden, I (1993). 'User expectations.' In *The responsible workplace* (ed. F Duffy, A Laing & V Crisp), Oxford: Butterworth Architecture/Estates Gazette, pp 16-32.

Lett, B (1993). 'Teleworking: an organic organizational development model for the 21st century.' *Library and Information Research News* 17 (58), pp. 15-18.

Lett, B (1994). 'Teleworking and the library of the future.' *Managing Information* 1 (4), pp. 27-29.

Library and Information Commission (1997). *New library: the people's network*. London: Library and Information Commission.

Lloyd, B (1993). 'The future of offices and work.' In *The responsible workplace* (ed. F Duffy, A Laing & V Crisp), Oxford: Butterworth Architecture/Estates Gazette, pp 44-54.

Luce, R E & Hartman, S (1984). 'Telecommuting to work: using technology to work at home.' *Library High-Tech* 2, pp. 79-83 (cited by Pinder, 1992).

Mack, L (1995). *Making the most of work spaces*. London: Conran Octopus.

Maitland, A (1998). 'Anyone working out there?' *Financial Times* 19 June, p. 13.

Moon, C & Stanworth, C (1997). 'Ethical issues of teleworking.' *Business Ethics* 6 (1), January.

Mowat, M (1998). *Legal liability for information provision*. London: Aslib.

Nicolle, L (1998). 'Teleworking/telecommuting.' *Financial Times* 19 June, pp. 15, 17.

Nilles, J M (1994). *Making telecommuting happen: a guide for telemanagers and telecommuters*. New York: Van Nostrand Reinhold.

Nilles, J M, Carlson, F R, Gray, P & Hanneman, G J (1976). *The telecommunications-transportation tradeoff*. New York: Wiley.

O'Leary, M (1987). 'The information broker: a modern profile.' *Online* 11 (6), pp. 24-30.

Paul, D (1996). *The home office book*. New York: Artisan.

Pinder, C (1992). *New patterns of work in librarianship*. M.Lib. dissertation. Aberystwyth: University of Wales

Scammell, A (1995). *The information needs of teleworkers in the financial services sector*. MA Dissertation, University of North London.

Scammell, A (1998). 'The virtual organisation.' *Online and CD Notes* 11 (9), pp. 3-4.

Sheehy, N & Gallagher, T (1996). 'Can virtual organizations be made real?' *The Psychologist* 9 (4) April, pp. 159-162.

Skyrme, D (1993). 'Flexible working – reaping the benefits.' In *The best of both worlds: how teleworking or distance working can benefit your organisation*. London: The Industrial Society.

Stanworth, C, Stanworth, J & Purdy, D (1993). *Self-employment & labour-market restructuring: the case of freelance teleworkers in book publishing*. London: University of Westminster.

Stanworth, J & Stanworth, C (1991). *Telework: the human resource implications*. London: Institute of Personnel Management.

Stonier, T (1990). 'Individual and domestic use of information.' In *Information UK 2000, British Library R&D Report 6020*, pp. 1-15, London: British Library.

Taylor, P (1998). 'Millennium will bring plenty of surprises.' *Financial Times survey: Office of the future*, 23 September.

Toffler, A (1981). *The third wave*. London: Pan.

Tomos, L (1997). 'The role of the public library within the wider context of public information systems: a case study of Wales. In *The Internet, networking and the public library* (ed. S. Ormes & L. Dempsey), London: Library Association Publishing/UKOLN, pp 13-23.

Vickers, P (1990). 'Information consultancy.' *Library & Information Briefings* 21. London: British Library.

9. Internet Resources

Web sites

Major sites with links to other sites

European Telework Online
http://www.eto.org.uk

Telework Telecottage and Telecentre Association
(TCA)
http://www.tca.org.uk

Writers and researchers

Analytica
http://dialspace.dial.pipex.com/town/parade/hg54/
(The director of Analytica is Ursula Huws, a
respected writer and researcher on teleworking)

Andrew Bibby
http://www.eclipse.co.uk/pens/bibby/telework.html

David Skyrme Associates
http://www.skyrme.com

Gil Gordon Associates
http://www.gilgordon.com

International telework organisations

Australian Rural Telecentres Association
http://www.arta.org.au

Belgium Teleworking Association
http://www.bta.be

Canadian Telework Association
http://www.ivc.ca/part2.html

French Telework Association
http://www.aftt.net

International Telework Association
http://www.telecommute.org/tachome.html

Irish Teleworking Association
http://www.iol.ie/tci

Netherlands Telework Forum
http://www.vifka.nl/ntf.htm

Portuguese Association for Telework Development
http://www.teleman.pt/apdt

Telecottages Sweden
http://www.telestugan.se/tcs/

Telecottages Wales
http://www.telecottages.org/default.htm

Telelavoro
http://www.mclink.it/telelavoro/

TELWISA
http://www.telewisa.de/

Teleworking Europa Forum
http://www.tweuro.com

Other useful sites

Association of Independent Information Professionals (AIIP)
http://www.aiip.org

BT Working From Home
http://www.workingfromhome.co.uk

Implementing Telework
http://www.telework-mirti.org

OwnBase
http://www.ownbase.org.uk

Tolson Messenger
http://www.tolsonmessenger.demon.co.uk

More URLs can be found in:

Blake, M, Cookman, N & Haynes, D (1999). *Teleworking directory*. London: British Library Science Reference Information Service.

10. List of Organisations

Active Information
Cribau Mill
Llanvair Discoed
Chepstow
NP6 6RD
Tel +44 (0) 1291 641 222
Fax +44 (0) 1291 641 777
Email info@better-business.co.uk
http://www.better-business.co.uk

Publishes a newsletter *Better Business* – formerly *Home Run* – that appears ten times a year. Originally it was aimed solely at home-based workers. With the name change in September 1998, it has widened its remit to include small businesses.

Aslib, The Association for Information Management
Staple Hall
Stone House Court
London EC3A 7PB
Tel +44 (0) 171 903 0000
Fax +44 (0) 171 903 0011
Email aslib@aslib.co.uk
http://www.aslib.co.uk

Source of training/professional development courses for LIS professionals.

Homelodge Buildings Ltd
Kingswell Street

Cranley
Winchester
Hampshire SO23 2PU
Tel+44 (0) 1962 881480

Provides timber buildings which could serve as offices.

Lawyers for Your Business
The Law Society
50-52 Chancery Lane
London WC2A 1SX
Tel+44 (0) 171 320 5764
Fax+44 (0) 171 831 0057
http://www.lawsociety.org.uk

The Library Association
7 Ridgmount Street
London WC1E 7AE
Tel +44 (0) 171 636 7543
Fax +44 (0) 171 436 7218
Email info@la-hq.org.uk
http://www. la-hq.org.uk

Publishes leaflets on Teleworking and Working from home.

Runs training courses for LIS professionals.

New Ways to Work
309 Upper street
London N1 2TY
Tel +44 (0) 171 226 4026
Fax +44 (0) 171 354 2978
Email nww@dircon.co.uk

A London-based charity that runs seminars and training sessions for employers and personnel officers. It publishes booklets, leaflets and a quarterly newsletter.

OwnBase, The National Association for Home Based Working
Birchwood
Hill Road South
Helsby, Cheshire
WA6 9PT
Tel +44 (0) 1928 723254
Email ownbase@coleman.u-net.com
http://www.ownbase.org.uk

Association providing a mutual support network to people working from home. Publishes a bimonthly newsletter.

Telework Telecottage and Telecentre Association (TCA, formerly the Telecottage Association)
Freepost CV2312
WREN
Kenilworth
Warwickshire CV8 2RR
Tel +44 (0) 1203 696986 or 0800 616008
Fax +44 (0) 1203 696538
Email teleworker@compuserve.com
http://www.tca.org.uk/

Foremost UK organisation for teleworkers. Publishes a bimonthly magazine, Teleworker.

TempleCo Ten Limited

Unit 5
Haslemere Industrial Estate
Weydown Road
Haslemere
Surrey GU27 1DW
Tel +44 (0) 1428 658383
Fax +44 (0) 1428 656370

Offers modular structures which act as self-contained workplaces.

UK Telework Platform
PO Box 16235
London
WC1N 2LT
Tel 0800 616 008
Email admin@telework.org
http://www.telework.org

Promotes the introduction of telework in businesses to increase their profitability and realise the environmental and social benefits of reduced travel and pollution.

For further details of organisations concerned with teleworking consult:

Blake, M, Cookman, N & Haynes, D (1998) *Teleworking directory*. London: British Library Science Reference Information Service.

Printed and bound by CPI Group (UK) Ltd, Croydon, CR0 4YY

17/10/2024

01775689-0002